ODD MAN OUT

ODD MAN OUT

Dennis Daly

MadHat Press
Cheshire, Massachusetts

MadHat Press
MadHat Incorporated
PO Box 422, Cheshire, MA 01225

Copyright © 2024 Dennis Daly
All rights reserved

The Library of Congress has assigned
this edition a Control Number of
2024932979

ISBN 978-1-952335-77-8 (paperback)

Words by Dennis Daly
Cover image: *Victorian man under streetlight in silhouette*
by Lee Avison
Cover design by Marc Vincenz

www.MadHat-Press.com

First Printing
Printed in the United States of America

Past Praise

The Custom House

Again and again, in poems of precision, conscience, and formal elegance, Dennis Daly arrests our vertiginous world so we may see its beauty, horror, and promise....
—Richard Hoffman, author of *Gold Star* and *Emblem*

Daly's book *The Custom House* is quite simply a force of nature and a powerful pleasure to read and re-read.
—Elizabeth Gordon McKim, author of *The Red Thread*

Night Walking with Nathaniel

Dennis Daly skillfully draws a vivid panorama of Salem, a town he knows profoundly well.... This is one of the more satisfying collections of American poetry in years, a generous array of deftly crafted work, memorable for its storytelling, imagery, and verbal music....
—X. J. Kennedy, author of *In a Prominent Bar in Secaucus*

In a time when other poets have forgotten the power of a metered witnessing of history, Daly brings a rare compassion to a community's misfortune and celebrates its dignity. These poems are precise, the lines embellished with a craftsman's beauty.
—Afaa Michael Weaver, author of *The Government of Nature*

Shield Wall

... [Daly's] classical learning and devotion to the heritages of poetry infuse but never dominate this collection. Time spent inside *Shield Wall* will take you from beginning points like "a riptide wraps around my heart," leading you down unexpected paths.
—David P. Miller, author of *Sprawled Asleep*

Sentinel

Dennis Daly's brilliant new collection, *Sentinel*, interrogates the very drive that has inspired it. The poet/interrogator, "Self's Iscariot," conducts an ars poetica waterboarding in which, "All must recant."

—Paul Pines, author of *Divine Madness*

In their cryptic allure and compelling density, the poems of Dennis Daly's *Sentinel* serve up a vision so dark, it achieves the paradox of blazing light upon the tormented psyche of protagonist after protagonist.

—Tomas O'Leary, author of *In the Wellspring of the Ear: New and Selected Poems*

Pantoums

Daly is unsparing in questioning life's paradoxes. By turn apocalyptic, by turn hopeful, Dennis Daly, through his artful pantoums, is the perfect guide for our anxious time.

—Pui Ying Wong, author of *An Emigrant's Winter*

Like Don Quixote, Dennis Daly, in *Pantoums*, sets off on a quest to manifest an impossible dream. In the poet's case, it's to realize an excellent book of poems, each of them written in the same, supremely challenging form. Unlike the knight of the baleful countenance, however, Daly succeeds.

—David M. Katz, author of *Stanzas on Oz*

The Devil's Artisan:
Sonnets from the Autobiography of Benvenuto Cellini

Daly perfectly captures the voice of a street-tough artist and courtier, a sculptor of heavy objects regularly on the lam. He meanwhile delivers an indelible landscape of Renaissance Italy and France—the courts, the palaces and the woodlands where goatish men roam.

—Rick Mullen, author of *Soutine*

Alcaics for Major Robert Rogers

… Daly employs the Greek poetic form of alcaic meter, used by poets like Horace and Tennyson. As a scholar, narrator, and poet, Daly challenges his readers and rewards them with delight and wisdom.

—E<small>D</small> M<small>EEK</small>, author of *High Tide* and *Luck*

Psalms Composed in Utter Darkness

In splendid and often poignant language, Daly's poems question the nature of free will, goodness, evil, justice, and mercy. These are haunting meditations on what it means to be human.

—D<small>ENISE</small> P<small>ROVOST</small>, Co-President of New England Poetry Club, and author of *City of Stories*

Other Books by Dennis Daly

The Custom House
Sophocles' Ajax: A Modern Translation
Night Walking with Nathaniel
Sentinel
21 Ghazels by Alisher Navoiy (translation)
Pantoums
The Devil's Artisan, Sonnets from the Autobiography of Benvenuto Cellini
Shield Wall
Alcaics for Major Robert Rogers
Psalms Composed in Utter Darkness

*For all the decent folk lost along the way—
family, friends, union allies, confidants, and fellow travelers*

Table of Contents

Identity

Identity	3
Around Salem's Common	4
A Sapphic Benediction for my Bar Mates at the Anchor Pub	5
Ankle Sprain at the Athenaeum	6
In the Cellar of the Beverly Depot	7
The Wreck of the *Britannia* in Salem Sound: November 1818	8
Buttered Rum	9
Crucible	10
Forgetfulness	11
Lost	12
Prescience	13
Change Order	14
Broken Router	15
An Ordinary Day	16
Vision	18

Odd Man Out

Odd Man Out	21
Separation	22
Near Exhaustion	23
The Harrowing of Hell	24
Upon Reading Christopher Marlowe's Massacre at Paris	25
Watchman	26
Dactylic Dust	27
Great Reckonings	28
Dalliance	29
Counterclaims	31
Mountain Snow	32
Fanatics	33
Mountain Tomb	34

Pottawatomie Killings — 35
Redemption — 36

God's Eyes

God's Eyes — 39
In the Beginning — 41
This Nativity — 42
Weather — 43
At Saint Mary's Monophysic Church in Diyarbakir, Turkey — 44
Falling Acorns and Morbidity — 45
Nobody — 46
Why Waltham Will Not Do — 47
Prayer for the Return of Dob Bosco's Brain — 48
Ode on Today's Canonization of Jacinta
    and Francisco Marto — 49
Terse Praise for X. J. Kennedy — 51
Epithalamium — 52
Uttered Dears — 53
Two Infants — 54
Musical Indirection — 55

String Theory

String Theory — 59
What, Still Alive at Sixty-six? — 60
Before the Big Bang — 61
Multiverse — 62
Heliopause — 63
In the Oort Cloud — 64
Two Jars — 65
Mountain Man — 66
A Dead Ringer — 67
Chance Meeting — 68
Political Advice — 69
Personal Politics — 70
Double Exposure — 71

Winter	72
Wild Words	73

The All-Souls Lounge

Ash Wednesday at the All-Souls Lounge	77
Beelzebub Buys a Round at the All-Souls Lounge	78
Boethius Has Second Thoughts at the All-Souls Lounge	79
Bypassing the All-Souls Lounge	80
Finding Joy at the All-Souls Lounge	81
Happy Hour at the All-Souls Lounge	82
Judgement Day at the All-Souls Lounge	83
Last Call at the All-Souls Lounge	84
Lilith Appears at the All-Souls Lounge	85
Lucky Day at the All-Souls Lounge	86
Mephistopheles Offers Advice and Insight at the All-Souls Lounge	87
Missing from the All-Souls Lounge	88
Playing Pinball at the All-Souls Lounge	89
Small Talk at the All-Souls Lounge	90
Acknowledgments	91
About the Author	93

*My looking ripens things
And they come toward me, to meet and be met.*
—Rainer Maria Rilke

IDENTITY

Identity

Parts of self here spin and there together
From sea-birthed mists or shafts from other suns.
Genesis continues like the weather.

Against the cold containment of leather
Leans a helix, a longing in fractions.
Parts of self here spin and there together.

Reset through centuries the bruised bother
Of love's anxious need combines, quickens.
Genesis continues like the weather

Over miles, or continents, or neither.
Passions mark the clash of wild seasons.
Parts of self here spin and there together.

Ether razors juiced up bolts, Oh brother!
Storms assault outer defenses, curl ribbons.
Genesis continues like the weather.

Fragments attract, under arcs they gather,
Mnemonic rags turned to serve as captions.
Parts of self here spin and there together.
Genesis continues like the weather.

Dennis Daly

Around Salem's Common

Around Salem's common anxious people pace,
They pause, look for the Devil in his tree.
The guile of love demands redemptive grace.

At all speeds they walk, the innocent race
As if hunted by those from whom they flee.
Around Salem's common anxious people pace.

No hills to distract; crushed rock is the base
Of the path from what was to what will be.
The guile of love demands redemptive grace.

Intentions correct emotions in space,
Arc beyond the bandstand immodestly.
Around Salem's common anxious people pace.

Circuits of life draw plodders to embrace
That suddenness of unpossessed beauty.
The guile of love demands redemptive grace.

Connections fray, diffuse without a trace.
Tears. Rawness of weather. Nothing to see.
Around Salem's common anxious people pace.
The guile of love demands redemptive grace.

A Sapphic Benediction
for my Bar Mates at the Anchor Pub

Drink your brew like Scythian horsemen, rudely
Quaffing blood from warrior skulls, boiled skinless.
Not to worry, bartenders bless our business:
Rounds keep on coming.

Dennis Daly

Ankle Sprain at the Athenaeum

Among the stolen books I missed
A step descending with drama
The stairs, beyond the abscissa,
Beyond space. This god-awful twist

That hasn't left after two weeks—
Asclepius, give me a break,
Some relief from this nagging ache
That alters my iambs, that tweaks

My rhymes into oblivion.
Send your messenger Morpheus
With agents of hocus-pocus.
Transform this downtime to action.

Isn't this always the problem,
A side-show of pleasure or pain?
Life imposes its suzerain
On art. Medicine daubs us numb.

In the Cellar of the Beverly Depot

Maelstroms of light pour over the stairs,
Torrents of new dread and antique fears.
Descending through the hidden pull,
Spectators come with drinks half-full.

Approvals encompass everyone,
Nods offered by rock-faced brethren
Grateful to host, to echo voices
Of bardic chant and muted choices.

Here imbalance has lost its control,
Retreated beyond this lone foxhole.
Ramparts exploding, shell after shell,
Our haven holds. Watch out for shrapnel.

Beneath this crust of peopled caverns,
Of pipes, of drains, of wiring concerns,
A sea of magma fills in a void,
Plates conflict, Lemuria destroyed.

This den centers the shake, the rumble,
The collapse of what needs to tumble.
Convulsion wands to life's plan a pause,
A generator without a cause.

The earth survives by Titan power,
Evident with each thundershower.
More wonders await within this shrine
As it sits aslant the Rockport line.

Dennis Daly

The Wreck of the *Britannia* in Salem Sound: November 1818

Hazards belie again life's next hurrah
As harbor shoals rise to meet disaster.
A brig sails into a blizzard's whipsaw.

Ill fortune brings to this crew a Jonah—
Albatross-man with mates and one master.
Hazards belie again life's next hurrah.

Under short sail, a blind twist, a grope, a yaw
Before the strike of wood on sandblaster.
A brig sails into a blizzard's whipsaw.

Eyelashes frozen, the sailor's lockjaw,
Lifeboats loosened; they launch all the faster.
Hazards belie again life's next hurrah.

The missing man roars in a beacon's draw,
Riding the jibboom. Death, always the jester!
Hazards belie again life's next hurrah.
A brig sails into a blizzard's whipsaw.

Buttered Rum

I fought on bunkered barricades
During sunshine's glare and blizzards,
Held pitchfork high, tossed live grenades
At boss-men and corporate wizards.

One day I fell, an oozing heap,
Those enemies surging through me.
I slid on past my old barkeep
"Buttered rum?" he asked insanely.

As earth spins on I do avow
My doubts on its revolutions.
Yet whetted axes do somehow
Cut knots. Weigh well these solutions.

Dennis Daly

Crucible

Heather-hearted, near wild we're born,
Attached to home and mother's coos.
The straying fills the fun of it,
Our eyes glint like future's news.

But skin we have in brutal games
Of cannibals and long-hut men.
We lose a finger here and there,
With dispensations granted then.

On return to approbation
At dawn we make the matter fine,
A molten mix, extruding words
That fashion artistry of mind.

So, from this harshness sons are born
And daughters to reset the stars.
Introductions damn us otherwise
To retroactive seminars.

Forgetfulness

Solar tempests hurtle in mightily
From a central flare of wind and plasma,
The world forgets from sea to shining sea.

Men lose their voices unexpectedly,
Their discs overwritten with new data.
Solar tempests hurtle in mightily.

Homes melt away in insecurity,
Continents collide in mindless trauma,
The world forgets from sea to shining sea.

Satellites swing wide all experts agree,
Computers convulsing with dementia.
Solar tempests hurtle in mightily.

Charged particles breed in proton algae,
Smother a grim pond with green nostalgia.
The world forgets from sea to shining sea.

They start again in our vicinity,
These children of men from flooded era.
Solar tempests hurtle in mightily,
The world forgets from sea to shining sea.

Dennis Daly

Lost

Arrival begs an awkward question—
What was lost along the forkless way?
Stalk the gift of shapeless fortune,
The spirit of self will never stay.

What was lost along the forkless way?
Both greenery and robin chirrups?
The spirit of self will never stay
Unless a certain snag develops.

Both greenery and robin chirrups
Bring smiles and hopes and canopy prayers,
Unless a certain snag develops,
As matters mount up, absorbing fears.

Bring smiles and hopes and canopy prayers,
Stalk the gift of shapeless fortune.
As matters mount up, absorbing fears,
Arrival begs an awkward question.

Prescience

We see ahead all that we've seen before,
The hurt that multiplies, the fear that spreads.
Waves roll in, the tide plunders more and more.

There's nothing here, of that we're pretty sure.
But watch your step, beware of copperheads.
We see ahead all that we've seen before.

Design the sky and fit it with a door.
As well it should, a guillotine beheads.
Waves roll in. The tide plunders more and more.

We win. We lose. We die. Who's keeping score?
The world is mad. We sorely need spare beds.
We see ahead all that we've seen before.

Our soldiers leave to fight a foreign war.
They bomb our foes, their trucks, their fields, their sheds.
Waves roll in, the tide plunders more and more.

The end is near, or so says our folklore.
Within each storm another storm embeds.
We see ahead all that we've seen before.
Waves roll in, the tide plunders more and more.

Dennis Daly

Change Order

Opposable thumbs be twice damned,
His resistant words he iambed.
Not that anyone would notice,
A comb-over trumped by baldness.

He stacked his lines as he must do
With run-on words like IOU
And stopped it all to edit stuff.
Would someone call the verse-sheriff?

There's ledge beneath his specked-out work,
A mystery to this ink-stained clerk.
He'll need to blast a bit more here
To stay endeared to Bill Shakespeare.

Broken Router

Surge of electric bolt
Blackened the insides, blew
The wires, burnt the rubber
Sheath firing up the power,

Letting odor trickle
Through space and time's curved sag.
Each idea falls away
Unconnected with carve

Of story; the adverbs
Lie gasping by the pool,
Space slides down viper's hole
Without especial pith.

Our audience awaits
In modem's soft expanse,
A universe adrift
From mused generation.

Dennis Daly

An Ordinary Day

Pray for a shining that may well happen,
Either aura rising to merge with sky
Or hitherto unmemorable blue.
Homer never understood the color
That tinted breathless visions of heaven
And masked the storm-tossing tidal fury.

Not that one should expect all-out fury.
Although, inscrutably, it does happen.
Earth, left behind, abandoned by heaven,
Makes do. Its denizens research the sky,
Build astrologies of lifelong color.
Prospects, perfuse, extend even to blue.

So, still we stand awash in sea-salt blue.
The hours about us bend in closed fury,
Our faces tint free of bloody color
As day gallops by. How does that happen?
Do Apollo's horses, trawling the sky,
Roll up the carpet of quantum heaven?

Sometimes a thought can burst into heaven,
Then catch us unaware, when waxing blue.
Silence seems to rule the cathedral sky
At those times, represses the fixed fury,
Interrupts disorder bound to happen.
Here truth totters, halting, without color.

Celebrations of love—Oh what color!
Each minute blessed in a fazed-out heaven,

Multiplying your face. It could happen,
Could fall apart, a blue on deep, deep blue,
A furtive smile before tempest fury.
Vows, like buttresses, hold in place the sky.

Daydreamed history fills the curves of sky,
Our time a blink of eternal color,
Lightning strikes, bolts of yesterday's fury.

Dennis Daly

Vision

Tempest-tilted I sit on lordly bench
At path's pebbled end and in fever rave
The early hours past pelt and drench of rain.
What electric sights cleave this plane of crows!

Gloam me soon. Spin into heaven's sparkle.
Open to vaults, to battering siege work,
To Uzziah's ballista fire that arced
Toward mud towers with sacerdotal rage.

Let come the exact, the imprisoned form,
Dormant in marble, mused over, ardent.
Let these hands fashion providential lines,
Conquer the known and hardened projections

Before dawn's masked aspect. Leviathans
Be damned. Winds temper. My words insurrect.

Odd Man Out

Odd Man Out

Amok they'll run. Over tea they'll plot
Forays of liberation. So, fife
And drum bring cheers, the heart's tommyrot
That taunts tyrant rule, the sharpened knife

Of order. Those boys will have their day,
Long dreamed, the reverence and the homage.
They'll come to know infernal foreplay
Like buttered turnips and boiled carnage.

Beware of multicolored daub-men
Who paint blood, who dime their brothers out
To tribal chiefs. Raiders comprehend
Old routes. They strike, flee, walkabout.

After the brawl one stumbles forward,
Burdened with foul sins of risen ghosts.
He turns face to sleet, his men bestirred
In misuse. He clings to life's lampposts.

Dennis Daly

Separation

Dart the feral anxious eyes,
The raddled fist thumps the flatland
Of dimension's inner lies.
Here impends the reprimand.

Clutch the fabric's molecules
Spread upon the pebbled shore.
Only acts of clowns or fools
Diverts one's loss to evermore.

Man the ghost ship's muted boards,
Search for lives that once held fast
With day's content and year's discords,
Below the stalwart mizzenmast.

Stop the breaths in frozen air
As gnaws uplift from love gone deep.
Advantage to the unaware
And those who often oversleep.

Near Exhaustion

Rundown, caved-in, unable to stand up
In the public square, answer those questions.
How many lost? Always one bottom line.
But here household gods forgive, forget the flawed,
The vanished men of midweek morning.

Shuffling will, must do. The soreness, the aches …
Those winds like sad notions hurtling by,
Hurried specters seeking a final rest,
A sinking in of who's won or who's failed
In the brace of life-guttering moments.

Not the solitary timelessness
Of completion, of a job so well done
That awards fly in from every corner.
Rather the drowsy half-steps that connect,
Besiege target cities, cut supply lines.

Dennis Daly

The Harrowing of Hell

Anesthetized in time's tepid glumness,
The doubts passed over them in bilious waves.
No speech among these lost and lovelorn ones,
Only the nods of God-forsaken shades,
Who rest for centuries against pillars
Or lounge before petroleum lagoons.

In this eerie ether neutrality
Inhabitants embolden each other,
Remember life's furious quickening
And the outrage of its cumulative chafe
That wore away birthrights of wonderment
Or scarred over miraculous blood-wounds.

Wise ones witness the explosive moment,
The quaking tomb spewing its bright colors
Of deep volcanic change and carnage.
A genetic river of molten zeal
Rages into Eden's gray wilderness.
Eve, bedazzled, eyes transfigured Adam.

Upon Reading Christopher Marlowe's *Massacre at Paris*

Power, near absolute, needs exercise,
Quiet wisdom, a pose that will not do.
Bloody tempers hide under every guise.

With swords and daggers nobles barbarize,
Since they're able. And it must continue.
Power, near absolute, needs exercise.

The words of sleuths dim the clearest of eyes
With new suspicions, with clue after clue.
Bloody tempers hide under every guise.

One watchword, one bell, the murderous cries
From life's killing fields, only the preview.
Power, near absolute, needs exercise.

Beware of all friends, beware of all allies
Who nod, who nudge, and rivals devalue.
Bloody tempers hide under every guise.

Directed deaths their origin defies.
Kingdoms collapse. Others rise in virtue.
Power, near absolute, needs exercise.
Bloody tempers hide under every guise.

Dennis Daly

Watchman

I dreamed I dreamt the world alive
In sleep this seemed to me a hive
Where men and women sought with speed
All that they sought, indeed, indeed.

Then vertically did smoke ascend,
Below I sat and stiffly penned
A memory of roil and flux,
Of furnaces and motor-trucks.

That was before the end of time
When poets spoke in pantomime,
And poisoned fruits were paramount
In garden hells of no account.

Beyond this dream within a dream
Delivered down my dread bloodstream,
The watchman of the night appears,
One farmer's helper sits and stares.

He sits and stares and holds that thought,
For workmen's lives aren't all hand-wrought.
No watchman ever startles him,
No archangel or synonym.

Awake I rise to treat the day,
Rerouted through the same doorway.
Within me lives night's awful space,
The WATCHMAN too in uppercase.

Dactylic Dust

After the collision, particles
Puckered and dried in the nuclear
Blur, in the remnant of earlier
Joys, just before the Bard's chemicals

Coughed into nothingness. Ink emptied
Wry broken words by the well of sprung,
Fabulous space as distressed high-strung
Ghosts gathered near, unaccompanied

Voices undone. So, so tenderly
Cornelia's breath dulls no looking glass.
Is all that lost? And the Mozart Mass,
Does that expire, wither weightlessly,

Bound for another inchoate core,
Birthed yet again on a meteor?

Dennis Daly

Great Reckonings

Back to each wall,
Eyes on the infernal door;
A quick stand-up precedes a fall:
An appellation ends without rancor.

Dalliance

Driven from his hearth and conflagrant home,
Aeneas found harbor, space for two hearts
And camped, put an end to his wanderings,
His tempest-wrongs and facades, he sought truth,
A glimpse of himself in another's eyes,
So licit in their longing's discontent.

From Carthage's walls, seemingly content,
Elders came, offered their sovereign's home.
But these elders he knew. With his own eyes
He named them, exalted their stalwart hearts,
Listened to their storm-wracked tales, saw the truth
In all they said. His mind wandering—

Back to Troy, before his forced wandering
Of the world began. Nor was he content
To have escaped to entangled truth,
At last meeting Dido. His only home
Now her palace where she calls those hearts
Who please her, drawn by her wide, fulgent eyes.

He sees new masts, new oars in Dido's eyes
And rigging too, a need for wandering
Through the wet world of mermaids and sea-hearts
In rash men, who will never be content
Until they birth Ilium a new home,
A civilization that barters truth.

But a woman's love holds a deeper truth.
She plies reveling nights and alchemist eyes

Dennis Daly

Of rapture. A forest cave serves as home
To feral beasts roughed up from wandering
By sudden hurly-burly. They content
Themselves there, scorn weather, shelter their hearts.

After passion ebbs from lovers, their hearts
Return to lonely destiny. The truth
Lies in delay. Aeneas must content
Himself to build a life with future eyes.
A sailor's charm, which steadies wandering,
He must forgo. He burns house. She burns home.

This tide upsurges truth in tears from eyes,
Withdraws content, leaves warring, wandering
Hearts, which may, through grief, find that other home.

Counterclaims

Lovers long for night, crave the day,
Not suffering heaven's absence,
Like wanderers from faraway
They thrill at meeting, at mergence.

Not suffering heaven's absence,
Note life's coercive exile,
They thrill at meeting, at mergence.
Yes, love revives the juvenile.

Note life's coercive exile,
Man's innocence notwithstanding,
Yes, love revives the juvenile,
Everything else is glad-handing.

Man's innocence notwithstanding,
Lovers devise love-centric games.
Everything else is glad-handing,
Except, of course, the counterclaims.

Lovers devise love-centric games
Like wanderers from faraway.
Except, of course, the counterclaims,
Lovers long for night, crave the day.

Dennis Daly

Mountain Snow

In micro-meteors sanded
From above, hell's heat-glow burns through
Season's frosted face like acid,

Moon-cratering these heights anew.
Blameless arcs, soft curves build themselves,
Shroud cannon, shells, war's residue

Beneath knitted crystal, ice-shelves
That glitter with indifference.
Beauty like this entreats, compels.

All squint-eyes search the assonance
For perfect cog and muffled wheel,
Calculate the cold white distance

Between organic and ideal.
Trucks line up before the tunnel,
Closed to all offerings mercantile.

Raw, mind-numbing stuff, man's nightmares
Driven to the last darkened pass,
Boxed neatly, antedating fears

Of vampire and vile incubus
Emerging from their frozen blocks
Under the flake-fall of epochs.

Fanatics

They lead children into oblivion,
Into the River Lethe. They stare elders
To vanishing points beyond their borders.
Timers are triggered. Hostages taken.
Lovers, fire-struck, awry, step off measures,
Bow to the sermons of severity
And gleam, the grim gleam of true believers.

They follow wild whirlwinds as they purge
The lax, the licentious geography
Of timeless vassals and arthritic men
Making their way through the dangerous check points.
Here beauty and goodness gulf, cancelled
Before the begun, the next calendar,
The opening book, the birth of Year One.

Mountain Tomb

Dead kings rule these sovereign heights.
Jezails fire at the sky, jubilate
Till dawn unveils their oversights
Of crumbled town. We contemplate

Faux empire and enemy mines
In calming fields, near cooling streams.
Still men of spark and stalwart spines
Will cross the river of extremes.

Civilizations rise again,
A children's game of tag, you're it!
Women warn of militiamen.
Skeletal guns we retrofit.

Pottawatomie Killings

About eleven o'clock I guided
Them across Mosquito Creek to the Doyle's
Cabin—you must understand he was
A prophet. "Ordained from eternity,"
He said.
        Taking father Doyle and two
Of his sons, we cut them to pieces
With broadswords while the mother and her youngest
Huddled in the corner of their home. I
Was trembling, ashamed—but he
Reminded us that one, "who sees not as
Men see," forgives the dark, terrible
Side of heroic struggles. Nevertheless
I don't sleep. The power of his righteous
Voice, "It matters not," drums through the night,
Correct and calculated. Sometimes I envy
The hesitation, the cowardice of most men.

Dennis Daly

Redemption

From the watchman at daybreak
Despair burns off into light,
Light into quiet redemption,
Love's waves wash over.

Wild grasses grown rigid with frost
Sense their loosened hold, their melt
Into the long dimensions,
The draft probing solace.

At once the whistles and world's buzz
Rollick in, a dance of breaths
And puckish jests stirring all,
One more liaison with life.

God's Eyes

God's Eyes

In the beginning before the ache,
Before the appalling sun collapsed,
Concussed the red and withered hill-scape,
His eyes blink twice, savor the unrushed

Moments. Window blinds bleed slotted light,
Covering her as she cooks her stew,
The onion, carrots, erudite
Herbs and meat chunks. Through his teleview

Of animal sense, recognition
Catches what wizards once called man's soul,
Projector of longing, fond notion
Beyond nature's selective control.

He memorizes each step, each burst
Breaking happiness, seizing his shore.
These lines she sings to him well-rehearsed
Over a marbled decade or more.

Eternal carnivore, conniver
Of our starlit firmament, he bends
To her aria, sparkled river
Pitching her notes forward. She transcends

All his creation's expanse, transforms
Severity into music's kiss.
Now a ghostly nudge in thunderstorms
Noses her awake. Times such as this

Dennis Daly

Belie our kind's origin and end.
Another blink, a lonely look surmised,
Transfixed forever, passed on, repenned
As wolf den, as home, as world reprised.

In the Beginning

Like a meteor firing the grottos
Of hidden space with ascendant startles,
With ethereal *ahs* and crystalline *ohs*,

You light up the mysterious angels
Rooted in my mouth, my hip bones, my chest.
I'm lifted beyond those drums and fiddles

And even windswept words. My thoughts caressed
Into country dawns and red tulip buds.
Earth bursts apart, greets what had been suppressed.

Once more they walk the earth, the druids
Of fertile being and ceremony.
I see them through you. Their runic methods

Proclaimed anew. Their ageless alchemy
Behind the drained faces of attraction,
The lure, the blind dazzle, the absentee

Whisperer of reason. Every dolmen,
Every sadness bows before the beacon
That cautions, warns of life's rapture again.

Dennis Daly

This Nativity

When star-clouds clutter the oldest of skies,
The moon bobs over the endless salt marsh
Carrying archives of crisp, pure silence
To inform once again the creation
Of ourselves in mankind's rudest stable.
Odors of oxen and sheep pervade the night,
Wrap with animal warmth perpetuity.
Cocksure, the camels stride the roll of steppes,
The Magi's gifts only moments away:
Gold, frankincense, myrrh, all in sealed caskets
Not to be opened, but only contained
Like multi-hued infectious maladies.
This nativity wreaths thought into itself.
Archangels gaze, intone Alleluias.

Weather

We wake to live in crazed weather,
A system of pressures that moves
Or stays. It normally behooves
Us to observe, then to answer
What the elements ask that day.
Do they casually hint and nudge
Or hurricane through with carnage
After their bilious breakaway?
In any case we need to meld
The neurons flitting deep inside
Our brains or minds (if that's implied)
With change that's wet and self-propelled.

Dennis Daly

At Saint Mary's Monophysic Church in Diyarbakir, Turkey

Here no one sees, presumes to know
Ancient bone and blood exceptions.
Haloed phantoms roam roundabout
Bestowing darkened ikon grace.

The priest parades his fervid pride,
Peoples a church with his children.
They praise paradise with giggles,
Their dreams still remote, still nascent.

Urban Savior, unconnected,
Not caressed by mortality
And the milky ages of love,
Keep marvelous this solitude.

Falling Acorns and Morbidity

The sky, indeed, is truly falling.
The end, my friends, is certainly nigh.
I'll soon be old and oddly aching
And buying liquor on the sly.

Oak trees now send another volley
To bruise us in our fragile lives.
They spy through leaves; their roots are crawly.
Our secret's out—no one survives.

Dennis Daly

Nobody

You're nobody saith Zelda,
You have not a Pulitzer Prize.
She's right! I'm only an elder
In the Church of Early Sunrise.

You have no right saith Zelda
To lecture our poet and queen
Who teaches workshops in gender,
Who writes like a Sapphic machine.

No, no you are not a worthy
You dare not question, not at all.
She's written oh so intensely
And fills up the festival hall.

So back, go back to your hovel
And cease your offensive onslaught
Saith Zelda, go now, grovel
To the poet-kings of Connaught.

Why Waltham Will Not Do

No, Waltham will not do,
Will not watch me walk on through,
Will not stop and chew the fat.
No. No. Not even that.

Waltham ticks, ticks to sleep,
Gives me dreams, counts all sheep.
Time's up! I'm told that too.
No. Waltham will not do.

Prayer for the Return of Don Bosco's Brain

Most squishy of relics purloined
From saints and their community
Of exposed members, grant redress.
For God's sake check the video!

Glass enclosed, you pondered yourself
Within that beloved fragment,
Or metaphysically alone
Above the cellular fray.

O patron of fussy editors
And publishing moguls (Who knew?),
Intercede, clue up the crime scene
Once so venerated, marked "stet."

May police set up quick roadblocks,
Recheck the routes of pilgrimage,
While others wait for ransom calls,
Bereft of holiness and hope.

Ode on Today's Canonization of Jacinta and Francisco Marto

May 13, 2017

When brother sun detached himself and spun
Above the milling flock at Fatima
Like a host, an unleavened confection
Held high, then zigzagging into drama,

Discalced Lucia marshaled her cousins close.
Under the offbeat, consternated skies
Rife with fresh secrets and innuendoes,
Weather evaporated lullabies.

I imagine a pope, the last Pius
Costumed within the Vatican Garden,
Consumed with prophetical animus,
A third message: revered desolation.

My mother understood. Our family prayed
Together before the living room's sofa,
Moved bead after bead over a decade
For peace, for the conversion of Russia.

The commies blinked, devolved, de-conflated
Into auctioneers, nuclear conmen.
Jacinta and Francisco outdated,
Died of influenza, age nine, age ten.

Dennis Daly

Apparitions erupt from innocence.
Today's womb opens, it comforts, endears.
Mary enters divinity's absence,
Miracles resolve into souvenirs.

Solar rays shine through a goblet's crystal.
Cerulean waters sparkle beyond joy,
Pour earthward from maternity's mantle.
Souls seek heaven. Eyewitnesses annoy.

Terse Praise for X. J. Kennedy

Oh Kennedy, what caused your pen to stray?
Yes, what would William Carlos Williams say?
The pound of that stress, the wink of that rhyme,
Your wry charming muse set the paradigm.
Lost scribblers, you led them from pharaoh's waste
Of straw-less mud-poems, you poker-faced
Old pirate. You posed non compos mentis
To grim souls, plotted not a little fuss,
Then stood back to watch as gates imploded,
With country-versed folk, each scene decoded.
Outlaws purloining metered craft soon proved
Your counter measures had begun, had moved
Those hidden relics from an ancient mound,
That melodic language once lost, now found.

Dennis Daly

Epithalamium

for Colleen

Eastern heights glossed by radiant power,
A palace of gold-leaf roofs in Thimphu,
Long lost horizons of sunlit virtue
Offer a tiger's nest, a lover's bower

Clinging to the sheer Himalayan cliffs
Of thrust-up seashells. Couples find berths here,
The fortunate ones. Time's dread auctioneer
Halted outside, blocked with allied plaintiffs

Who grow laborious sleights into grudges
Or piqued pedestrians, named, then accused,
Their brickbats and wrangles forever fused
Together. This realm forbids such carnage.

May you, my chic daughter, and your Colin
Find adventure among the tiptop summits
That preserve tall lands from probing bandits
And electric bolts beyond our heaven.

May you both see in your goblet crystal
Star-tears of mirth, calm, and comforting glints
As you find again and follow the footprints
Of family lines, of lords and damsels

Hidden in memory's unexplored pages.
There stride the Patagonian penguins
Hand in hand with those benevolent djinn,
Who guard you still, grant your dearest wishes.

Uttered Dears

Whose dreams can find these bits of words
In curl of spume, in drive of tide
Beyond the drift of vague rewards,
Beyond the orbital divide?

Let them collect and cull these things,
A holy grail of syllables,
And draw them in, enclose with wings
My uttered dears, my valuables.

Dennis Daly

Two Infants

for Tristan and Eveleen

Angels swoon, flit
Before these newborn eyes
In the blossoms of afternoon.
Mothers cuddle, sit—
Dear, dear those skies,
Above the pulse of bird tune.

Babes, engulfed in light,
Suck in a world of glint.
In the blossoms of afternoon
Believe no other right,
Just cooing sound or soleprint,
Just life, so lovingly spooned.

Musical Indirection

Our gravities rush down, rush out,
A universal waterspout
Inverted into heavy rain.
This flood will fill my next quatrain.

String Theory

String Theory

We drift apart in outer space
With other flotsam tumbling there.
The life we knew we can't replace,
Those broken shapes beyond repair.

With other flotsam tumbling there,
Some batteries, some bricks, some books,
Those broken shapes beyond repair,
Our selves affixed to tenterhooks.

Some batteries, some bricks, some books,
Hard prompts once promised constancy.
Our selves affixed to tenterhooks,
Details segment in open sea.

Hard prompts once promised constancy,
Your love was anchored in those things.
Details segment in open sea,
Up-down forces tug my heartstrings.

Your love was anchored in those things,
The life we knew we can't replace.
Up-down forces tug my heartstrings.
We drift apart in outer space.

Dennis Daly

What, Still Alive at Sixty-six?

What, still alive at sixty-six,
Not ever crossed the river Styx?
You measured, wrote, and saw things once,
Yes, had a kind of clairvoyance.

Mind and mouthed word could not keep up.
You lay there like a smashed turnip
As years recede, they seethe away:
A life constructed of cliché.

The Afghan mountains hide enough,
They mask murder and cloaked mischief.
You wandered there to find life's view
And found that lost world rhymed. Some do.

Before the Big Bang

Billowed the wind of Ur-forces
Through the murk murmurs and gloom motes
A firmament folds in, connotes
The inflated idea. Auras,

Too thin, expand into nowhere,
Capture hints of particle smidge,
Spreading over spatial cordage.
Shadows move in, something aware

Resonates, pours out energy
Sating the source behind the source,
The smooth agate, a universe
Concave, a coerced prodigy.

Dennis Daly

Multiverse

Iambs embubbled search out all that you
Are or were ever to me bumping here,
Bumping there, a lifetime one can't undo
Nor would. The punctuation of love rare

In this thoughtless age or any other.
Each line of longing stress connects, hangs on
Through the madness of ignited weather:
A lover's promised tryst, a world reborn.

Heliopause

Before the frozen fireworks
The shooting up of Oorts' frontier,
I come awake among the clerks
Of pitch and sales and easy sneer.

I come awake to count the days
In cobblestones of erstwhile space
Then set my temporal earth-bound gaze
On things undone, on odd typeface.

Supplicants beg biographies
When soon they exit into sleep
And tune in to those frequencies
That urge me on, beyond knee-deep.

I rage alive in foreign realm,
Denounce all detritus of stress.
The winds die down, I underwhelm
In this the game of effervesce.

Dennis Daly

In the Oort Cloud

Far from the heliosphere frozen sparks,
Tails trailing on the interstellar edge,
Near collide with other shooting landmarks
Here today, gone with tomorrow's knowledge,

Arcing through the troubled minds of Magi
Trekking the calamitous dessert routes
In search of perfections that versify
Themselves, eliminating lifelong doubts.

Everywhere omens of new creation
Whisper their glad inscrutable warnings
To breathless crowds. A moment's digression
Births to being on a cradle of strings.

Two Jars

after Avianus

A wild current rushed
Us off a riverbank, two jars
Caught in a season's tumult.
We bobbed and twirled in a fall back,
Catch-up harmony.

Different craftsmen created us: you
Of fused bronze with a brilliance
Drawn from the sun, and I
Of molded clay, thinly glazed,
Brittle.

You promise distance; your
Metallic exterior always a threat
To me. We circle in a silent dance.
A dance until tears come. Or
A closing in for the kill.

Dennis Daly

Mountain Man

Day rests rebellion in whiskey-numb whirl,
The certitude of snow, a curve of drift.
In him no steadiness, a constant shift
Confronts nag's nonesuch, the whisper, the churl.

Below the mountain tops, above the sky
He ranges the world, sets his steel contraptions,
Where creeks conjoin to blossom sand barrens,
Where creatures cringe the wolf-fang, the hawk-eye.

Mounds of pelts payroll him for future kills,
Knead down the rage of loss, the seared muscle.
Tomahawk ready, his secrets unrevealed,

Here he stands over pressed and twisted wills,
Shadow-smothered by withered oracle,
Drawn to plateau of flames, combusting field.

A Dead Ringer

A dead ringer for Bill Hickok, he sat,
His back to the door, drew three cards, winced.
Everyone sipped their beers, waiting.
I hazarded a word in consolation,
But I doubt if he heard me. He had known
All along: the suspicion, the abeyance
Of anger, the set up. Even my part:
To get him there. And why should friendship
Interfere? Suddenly, footsteps on the porch.
We stood up, moved away from the table
Determined to see this through. Without
Expression he considered a bluff, saw
It wouldn't work, discarded it. He sat
There forsaken, resolute. God! I wanted
To live like that; to take his place.

Dennis Daly

Chance Meetings

I passed you by as if in jest
As if I did not understand
The gift of love or even guessed
The numbered grains of desert sand.

I passed you by, nor did I count
Those other times, betwixt, before.
Some words were said. I have no doubt
I heard them in my very core.

I did not pass you by again.
I stopped as you crisscrossed to me.
The gap now bridged from there to then.
In this life lies infinity.

Political Advice

Beware of tyrants like Macbeth.
Don't work for them. You'll catch your death.

Dennis Daly

Personal Politics

Party politics are worrisome enough,
Infused with our troubles, it's toxic stuff.

Double Exposure

One layer, one switchback raises
Checkpoints that settle in, appear
To wary pilgrims, who travel
Over these peaks, stark and airless.

We imagine, wedged, jammed
Into our just lowered windows,
Terse guns, eyeing our jaw-movement,
Suspicious of a finger twitch,

A rolling tongue. Though we expect
The worst, the vehicle that blocks
Our flight fades, finger-smudged away
Under the next mused up stratum.

We drive through the apparition
Heading north. A tunnel offers
To forgive transgressors, exacts
A penance of oblivion.

Dennis Daly

Winter

Daylight's revolution drops off the earth
Amid questions best left for one's next birth.
While blizzard bands build up the glacier's mass
A civility dies with each trespass
Against concord, nod to intuition,
Cartons of neatly stacked ammunition.

Look to it! Look to it! The season's ice
Anesthetizes, blurs this paradise
Fit for vipers. Man reintroduced them
In the autumn. It was the stratagem
To nudge the plan, to unnerve the lot
Beyond the wind shift, in counterplot.

Wild Words

Wild words whirling in the gasps of fish gill,
Wanton gales wambling under birch branches,
Remembered days in creation's gristmill

Ground out as heartaches that hind sights instill
With strikes of light and reversal flashes—
Wild words whirling in gasps of fish gill.

In open fields we wait for wisdom's fill.
Tongues afire with fervor fall to ashes:
Remembered days in creation's gristmill.

Touch of lovers, the lean of daffodil
Into the multiples of mishmashes—
Wild words whirling in the gasps of fish gill.

When glaciers inch down, a gnaw, a prechill
Into snow drifts' glare with iced eyelashes,
Remembered days in creation's gristmill.

Times expire with man's faith and freewill
Loudly alive despite those backlashes,
Wild words whirling in the gasps of fish gill,
Remembered days in creation's gristmill.

The All-Souls Lounge

Ash Wednesday
at the All-Souls Lounge

Dust to dust, my bar mates celebrate
This Lenten exit from life's drama.
We wear a smudge, curb our gluttony
That would transform our natural selves,
Speed the slaughter of our fellow beasts
And lead to further temptations.
Funereal gloom fuels this gathering
Of desperate travelers, who tip well,
Who play this singular star-crossed pause
For all it's worth in grace and leverage.

Fat Tuesday's aftermath grifts us in
To this dour conclave of sparsity,
One grade above a destitution,
A taunt of game's end or nearly that.
The God-forsaken gall of it all
Gleans through as we drink away the night,
Lament the sins of imperfection
As we recite the priestly penance
Given us. Words change into clocks.
The shortest hand points the way back home.

Dennis Daly

Beelzebub Buys a Round at the All-Souls Lounge

Thunderbolts outside for peak drama,
A boilermaker raises me up
To a higher sphere. The TV on.
Time's penitent will soon appear
Seeking himself in this cursed place,
Haven from torment and emptiness.
What's wrong? asks the disembodied voice
Telecast from above. I measure
My own cause, lose articulation,
Stare at the face of dolor and dread.

High Principalities rain down shafts
Of star-madness, leaving the distraught
No escape. Beelzebub walks in,
Buys a round—for myself and three others.
I'm identified with a slight nod
And, seemingly, well-meant deference.
Thinking ahead through some confusion
I pivot toward the door— tightly shut,
Look to my despair. His aspect
Gloams us in this, our fool's paradise.

Boethius Has Second Thoughts at the All-Souls Lounge

Self-pity by poet never sells,
Which doesn't surprise since set meter
Feeds the attic bugs, book by sorry book.
"A double ... yes, barkeep, another,"
Says Boethius, "I am banished
From my stable aspect." At the bar's end
A woman looks over. "Come on," she says,
"Grief clouds your mind with doubt,
Order triumphs among us drinkers,
Justice must confound wickedness."

"Confound! That's one way of putting it,"
Answers the Consolation's author,
"The machinery of fate grinds on,
With good outcomes and bad." An uproar
Breaks out at one of the side tables.
A glass of ale spills. "Vice often wins
Within the mysterious wheeling
Of stars," he continues with some bother,
"Yet happiness persists in this place
Beyond time and our understanding."

Dennis Daly

Bypassing the All-Souls Lounge

Not tonight. The bloody-red façade
Of daubed brick, unshakably infixed
Into a floating mercantile strip,
Which twirls forth through the constellations,
Does not appear. The walk alone calms,
Solaces those keen ingrown hurts
That wake one from the soundest of sleeps
And nags the restive body to rise,
To pace into the small witching hours,
Devoid of superfluous noises.

Not tonight. Needed wits conjure up,
Face off the abysmal denizens,
The gargoyles dimmed in opacity,
In nocturnal murk. Here truth wills out,
Corrects courses for tomorrow's use.
Only then will words bear strength again,
Find new bearings between slanted poles
And more temperate geographies.
Only then will occult concoctions
Lure one into another respite.

Finding Joy at the All-Souls Lounge

An outpost that deeply prods the universe.
It takes the odd ones and the wastrels,
Who, lost, seek direction down dead-end streets.
Here the crisscross chatter of grave patrons
Sends out dark waves of mid-ocean madness.
Watch how the barmaid defers to those tables
They tightly share, drinks dutifully served.
But it's not just the alcohol. Chairs float
Past us, transport through space droll oracles
Of the moment, divining better days.

In this secreted man-of-war cabin
The once dead and soon-to-be-born
Study methods of everlasting life.
Mnemonic skills branded in the helix,
Doubled and dateless, of our stout species.
Applause breaks the blather. A gamed event
Pours into the void, a recognition
Not to be missed, an earthly connection
With human merit and distinctive strength.
Come revelry of blessed consciousness.

Dennis Daly

Happy Hour at the All-Souls Lounge

Vivid sparks shoot out everywhere,
The ethereal smithy slams
Down his fundamental hammer
As I sip my jar of whiskey
And nod to that sweat-veiled forger
Of well-oiled Damascus steel,
A quickening sword telecast.
Moving toward me, the barkeep smirks
Then smiles his all-knowing welcome.
I'm early and unrepentant.

From spatial mist others drift in,
Fired metal moved aside with tongs.
A hilt with pommel now fashioned
While draft beers or iced drinks are poured,
Pockets sapped of greenbacks and coins.
Some talk on tomorrow's subjects,
Some keep their peace, their weighted hearts
Self-contained, losing harsh detail.
The fine file and whetstone applied
To blade's edge, creation's prelude.

Judgment Day at the All-Souls Lounge

At the crack of God-configured doom
The walls come down, expose the hidden
Trespassers, air out the waiting rooms.
Here the patient folks cool off, await,
All regulars having assembled,
Eternal and redundant verdicts,
Each binary configuration
Chiseled in our transcendent ether.
Afire with insight this new sphere blooms
A radiance enveloping all.

Everywhere the hurt and hurried rise
To meet a redo of their lost selves.
A quantum video replicates
The moments. Non-drinkers sip coffee
From cracked cups. Freshly ordered cocktails
Are poured by the barman, then garnished.
Innocence permeates this nexus
Of universes. Alleluia.
Generations shout alleluia.
Our world has begun again. Drink up.

Dennis Daly

Last Call at the All-Souls Lounge

Life requires one's final order.
We wait, spent with mob riot and wince,
With wide-eyed fear that creeps with demons
Faced once too many times, awful times,
Times remembered with tremors of age.
The barman delivers the hard drinks
That exit needs: the well-buttered rum
Of years past, the tapped mugs of lager,
The margaritas, stung with sea salt
Rimming the glasses of clueless youth,

And single or double shots of whiskey
For the hardened loners, who travel
By their wits. Our untethered lounge docks
Onto the darkened territory
Of bait and switch, of visages burned
Without recognition or the cache
Of mindfulness. These granular shores
Forbid the boots of forgotten wars
Yet to be fought by the soon fallen.
We get up, leave, enter a new world.

Lilith Appears at the All-Souls Lounge

Shape-shifting Lilith tongues the sea salt
From her lime-clogged margarita.
She's tarried here from the beginning,
Offering those freshly picked apples,
Her garden's best, and neatly drinking
In a storm of built-up reverie.
She observes us with her clan's hunger,
Luring men in with her pellucid charms,
Nourishing their exotic ruins.

The course of history has moved on,
Left this woman lost to time's ravage,
Alone, but with powers intact,
Still engorged, still illegitimate.
Her fidgets beyond the cosmic walls
Cross deep trenches at the origin.
Through the night she flings animal howls,
Fires the star-scape, the launched universe.
But first she comes to this bar to brood,
Bruit gossip with her earth-bound mates.

Dennis Daly

Lucky Day at the All-Souls Lounge

Time to forget life's dribs and awful drabs
And seal up the essential directions,
The back seat voices that nudge you forward,
Despite the obvious hesitations
Of others. No worse for wear, you're ready
To take your place, to grow into yourself,
To redo your most magnificent sins.
Then goodness will gush through every motion
You make. Every nod. Every common tic.
Guides will swoon, defer to you. Teacher's pet.

But today, bare, and full of eloquence,
You ready yourself in blasts of silence.
"Who are you?" asks the quaking universe
Before the final tug. Look to the light,
Look, don't think at all. Your cause and effect
Will kick in and another ride begin.
Soon enough you'll leave for the nether lands
Where tactful bartenders, schooled to govern,
Gather their sedentary customers,
Proffer drinks, always on the house.

Mephistopheles Offers Advice and Insight at the All-Souls Lounge

"Life need not be brutish and short,
Interrupted only by madness.
Over here. Hey. House gin and tonic,"
Huffs Mephistopheles, "and keep them
Coming." The barman's nod his answer.
"Power breeds pleasure, and much favor,"
The hellion continues, "each blessing
Brings with it a curse. It's brisk business!
Opportunity demands quick wit
Paired with a grasp of steely command.

Correct human nature, give order
To chaos. Feed the hungry with bread
And meat. That's the way of haloed saints.
Also, the way of mortal sinners."
More drinks queued for Mephistopheles,
Delivered with grand insouciance.
He smacks his lips, "They who admonish
Or flatter you are of the same ilk.
Without both genii this enchanting blink
Would cease and humanity conclude."

Dennis Daly

Missing from the All-Souls Lounge

George's stool, the one no one will sit on.
Long time empty. But overlaid, weighted.
For years his refuge from memory,
From Okinawa, its human carnage.
Thirty years back. Or, alternatively,
One hour ago. Is mankind truly steeped
With bloodlust. A jeep full of pinched spirits
Distilled from the River Lethe he conveyed
To safety, the POW camp
Guarded by Leo his Seabee brother.

Does brutality die in the jungles
Of engagement? Do flame-throwers burn
Away all residue of resistant flesh?
Even Leo, who ditched his uniform
In a dumpster, has trekked beyond his beer
And cigarettes to mnemonic repose.
Still, the stool will, in time, be occupied
By a queue of fools, of silly drinkers,
Who deny the truth of their own nature,
Who counterfeit the next generation.

Playing Pinball
at the All-Souls Lounge

Plunged into the busy, bitter world
Of jackpots and double bonuses,
My life, like a silver ball, flutters
Afield, nudged offbeat, irregular.
Its descent, too swift, much too dizzy
For its own good, ends with a new launch
Into the bumpers, collecting points,
Caroming up, controlling nothing.
Flippers in readiness, the tilt threat
Beyond my ken of outside strategies.

Three bright orbs or opportunities
In this brutal life. Watch the display.
As we age, the machine makes changes,
Values appreciate or dissolve.
We see it in some flummoxed faces
While they calculate goodness by score.
Learn to hold one's fate on a flipper,
A momentary rest, a comma
To vicissitudes, mindful or not.
Then send the ball on toward completion.

Dennis Daly

Small Talk at the All-Souls Lounge

Buzz words bound into the universe
Of wooden bar and circular stools,
Syllable shreds sounding out deep space
Between transients and their lagers.
One wonders aloud at the boldness
Of their predations or predictions.
Will there be a lightning strike tomorrow?
Will cities flood with incoming tides?
They drink their spirit miscellany,
Brace for the fierce tongues of prophesy.

Too many seats filled by babblers,
Who would right the tottering nation
If needed. A new agenda of replacements—
Hips and knees guaranteed to succeed.
Doctor such and such avers robots
Are on the move, they reflect themselves.
Another, here, I point at my jar,
Its contents imbibed. A memory
Misplaced already. Others follow.
I take a breath, breathe in an aura.

Acknowledgements

Constellations: A Journal of Poetry and Fiction: "Two Infants," "Before the Big Bang," "Redemption"

Muddy River Poetry Review: "Mountain Man," "Two Jars," "A Dead Ringer," "Vision," "Pottawatomie Killings"

Lyrical (Somerville Times): "Odd Man Out," "Nobody"

Molecule: "Great Reckonings"

The Asses of Parnassus: "Political Advise," "Personal Politics," "Falling Acorns and Morbidity," "Musical Indirection," "A Sapphic Benediction for my Bar Mates at the Anchor Pub," "Why Waltham Will Not Do"

Ibbetson Street: "Terse Praise for X. J. Kennedy," "The Harrowing of Hell," "Epithalamium," "An Ordinary Day," "Judgement Day at the All-Souls Lounge," "Upon Reading Marlowe's *Massacre at Paris*"

Bagels with the Bards Anthology: "Ankle Sprain at the Athenaeum," "Prayer for the Return of Don Bosco's Brain"

Wilderness House Literary Review: "Ode on Today's Canonization of Jacinta and Francisco Marto," "At St. Mary's Monophysic Church in Diyarbakir, Turkey"

Lily Poetry Review: "Lilith Appears at the All-Souls Lounge"

The Lothlorien Poetry Journal: "Playing Pinball at the All-Souls Lounge," "Bypassing the All-Souls Lounge," "Ash Wednesday at the All-Souls Lounge," "Boethius Has Second Thoughts at the All-Souls Lounge

North of Oxford: "Happy Hour at the All-Souls Lounge"

Life in New England Anthology (Swan Hope Press): "Around Salem's Common"

About the Author

DENNIS DALY lives in Massachusetts with his wife, Joanne. They have four adult children. Daly graduated from Boston College and earned an M.A. in English Literature from Northeastern University. He has previously published ten books of poetry and poetic translations. Among other jobs Daly has worked as a dockworker, a union leader of a 9000-member industrial local, a city department head, and a community corrections director. He has traveled widely in central Asia. Please visit his blog here: dennisfdaly.blogspot.com.

www.ingramcontent.com/pod-product-compliance
Lightning Source LLC
Chambersburg PA
CBHW020336170426
43200CB00006B/400